BIBLE POEMS

Events, People and Passages

By

Doris J. McMillan

ISBN: 0-7596-7942-8 (e-book)
ISBN: 0-7596-7943-6 (Paperback)
ISBN: 1-4033-1312-1 (Hardcover)

This book is printed on acid free paper.

1stBooks - rev. 06/14/02

Biblical information and scriptural quotations are taken from the Authorized King James Version of the Holy Bible.

DEDICATION

To the Lord God Almighty, His Son
Jesus Christ and the Holy Spirit Who gave me strength and knowledge
to write these poems; I give praise, glory, and honor.

To

Antioch Missionary Baptist Church of Goldsboro, North Carolina
and its members

And

Special recognition to the Sunday School members who listen to my poems read
in class, and inspired me to continue with poetry writing.

In memory of my grandparents
Reverend Henry Thomas and Fannie Johnson Hopkins
My parents
Nehemiah and Bertha Davis
My nephew
Rudolph (Buster) Davis

Special recognition
To
My Son
Marshall Wayne White
My sisters and brother
Pearl Adams, Fannie White, Louise Garrett, and Nehemiah Davis, II

TABLE OF CONTENTS

INTRODUCTION xiii

THE OLD TESTAMENT

THE CREATION 3
ADAM AND EVE 4
NOAH 5
TOWER OF BABEL 6
SODOM AND GOMORRAH 7
ABRAHAMS'S COVENANT 8
ABRAHAM'S TEST OF FAITH 9
ESAU AND JACOB 10
JACOB'S VISION OF A LADDER 11
JACOB'S NAME CHANGED TO ISRAEL 12
JOSEPH SOLD INTO EGYPT 13
JOSEPH INTERPRETS THE DREAM 14
JOSEPH REVEALS HIMSELF TO BROTHERS 15
MOSES, THE BEGINNING 16
MOSES AND THE BURNING BUSH 17
MOSES AND THE RED SEA 18
JOSHUA 19
DEBORAH AND BARAK 20
GIDEON 21
SAMSON 22
RUTH AND NAOMI 23
ISRAEL REQUESTS A KING 24
HANNAH, MOTHER OF SAMUEL 25
DAVID ANNOINTED KING 26
DAVID AND GOLIATH 27
SOLOMON 28
DIVIDED HOUSES 29
JEROBOAM'S IDOLS 30
ELIJAH MEETS THE WIDOW WOMAN 31
ELIJAH HEALS THE WIDOW'S SON 32
NABOTH'S VINEYARD 33
JEZEBEL AND KING AHAB 34
NAAMAN HEALED FROM LEPROSY 35
REBUILDING THE TEMPLE 36

NEHEMIAH.. 37
ESTHER AND MORDECAI... 38
JOB'S TEST: POSSESSIONS LOST 39
JOB'S FAITH: POSSESSIONS RESTORED 40
THE SECRET PLACE OF GOD.. 41
ISAIAH'S VISION OF THE LORD.. 42
BROKEN CLAY BOTTLE 43
BESIEGE OF JERUSALEM 44
EZEKIEL 45
VALLEY OF DRY BONES 46
MESCHACH, SHADRACH & ABEDNEGO............................ 47
DANIEL INTERPRETS THE KING'S DREAM........................ 48
DANIEL INTERPRETS THE HANDWRITING ON THE WALL.................... 49
DANIEL IN THE LIONS' DEN... 50
JONAH... 51
TITHES AND OFFERINGS.. 52

THE NEW TESTAMENT

BIRTH OF JESUS.. 55
SHEPHERDS TOLD OF JESUS' BIRTH................................. 56
WISE MEN FOLLOW THE STAR TO BETHLEHEM 57
JOHN THE BAPTIST.. 58
JESUS TEMPTED BY THE DEVIL... 59
MAN WITH UNCLEAN SPIRIT 60
JESUS, THE POWERFUL HEALER.. 61
PARALYZED MAN.. 62
MAN WITH THE WITHERED HAND 63
PARABLE OF THE SOWER 64
MAN WITH A LEGION OF DEVILS 65
JARIUS' DAUGHTER 66
WOMAN SICK FOR TWELVE YEARS.................................. 67
DEAF AND DUMB MAN... 68
GREATEST APOSTLE 69
RICH YOUNG MAN... 70
JESUS' RIDE INTO JERUSALEM 71
JESUS IN THE TEMPLE 72
POOR WIDOW WOMAN... 73
SIGNS OF CHRIST'S COMING 74
ELISABETH, MOTHER OF JOHN THE BAPTIST 75
THE GOOD SAMARITAN.. 76

MARY AND MARTHA 77
THE TEN LEPER MEN 78
BOASTFUL RICH MAN 79
THE PRODIGAL SON 80
LAZARUS AND THE RICH MAN 81
ZACCHEUS 82
FIRST MIRACLE OF JESUS 83
NICODEMUS 84
THE SAMARITAN WOMAN 85
THE HELPLESS MAN 86
JESUS FEEDS FIVE THOUSAND 87
LAZARUS RAISED FROM THE DEAD 88
BELIEVE IN THE LORD JESUS CHRIST 89
THE ANNOINMENT OF JESUS 90
THE CRUCIFIXION OF JESUS 91
THE RESURRECTION OF JESUS 92
ASCENSION OF JESUS 93
DESCENT OF THE HOLY SPIRIT 94
PETER HEALS A LAME MAN 95
ANANIAS AND SAPPHIRA 96
PETER'S MIRACLE IN JOPPA 97
PAUL'S CONVERSION 98
PAUL AND SILAS 99
PAUL AT MARS HILL 100
ARMOR OF GOD 101
OUR HIGH PRIEST 102
JESUS, THE SACRIFICE 103
FAITH 104
THE NEW JERUSALEM 105

INTRODUCTION

In July 1997, the Antioch Missionary Baptist Church held its Adult Vacation Bible School Class under the direction of Mrs. Vernetta Smith, and teachers, Reverend Charles Franklin and Sister, Lettye Clark.

The subject for one of the classes was: "God's Promises in Times of Financial Stress." The scripture was taken from I Kings 17:1-6. The students were given one line of a limerick ending with the word, "money," and were told to complete the remaining four lines. I wrote a few limericks, and read them to the class and teachers who seemed to enjoy them. It was then with the encouragement of my teachers, and director, I developed an interest in poetry writing. Later, in Sunday school, I summarized lessons taught by Reverends John Harrington and Charles Franklin, in poetry.

Writing biblical poems have comforted me more than words can express. It is my wish and desire that these poems will bring enjoyment and happiness to all who read them. At the close of our Vacation Bible School, a program was presented, and the following poem was read as tribute.

There were two teachers named Charles and Lettye,
Who with another teacher and director named Vernetta;
Gave students a new outlook
On lessons from the Great Book,
In Antioch's Vacation Bible school working faithfully together.

THE OLD TESTAMENT

Doris J. McMillan

THE CREATION

When God began earth and heaven creations,
The world was dark, had no form or population;
Then God said let there be light
And divided the day from the night;
With the sun, moon, and all the constellations.

God placed the firmament called heaven above the Seas,
And the earth, He called dry land to yield grass and trees;
After making all moving creatures, fowls, and great whales
And in His own image, male and female;
He rested, saw His creation as good, and was pleased.

Genesis 1

Doris J. McMillan

ADAM AND EVE

After God created Adam and Eve,
He placed them in a beautiful garden of fruit trees;
He gave them instructions
The tree of knowledge if touched, will bring destruction;
The Garden of Eden was their home to stay, not to leave.

Now there was someone else in the garden,
Whose heart was evil and harden;
A serpent, the devil in disguise
Told the woman: "Eat from this tree, and you will be wise."
Adam and Eve disobeyed God, and did not get a pardon.

Genesis 1,2,3

NOAH

God commanded Noah to build an ark,
Of wood from the gopher tree, not the bark;
He gave him the instructions
How to begin the ark's construction;
And built it according to God's fashion and mark.

Noah and his family went into the ark when it began to rain,
Also two of every living thing, male and female kind and strain;
When they went in as God commanded him
The Lord closed the ark's door and shut them in;
And the waters increased, covering all earth and plain.

It rained upon the earth for forty days and night,
The flood waters prevailed, no land could be seen in sight;
When the water receded from the deep of its fountain
The ark rested upon Ararat's mountain;
After a hundred and fifty days of the floods plight.

Noah sent a raven, and then a dove to search,
For dry land, but only the dove returned, it could not perch;
After seven days, he again sent the dove out
It returned with an olive leaf in its mouth;
Then Noah, his family, and all living creatures came out upon dry earth.

Genesis 6:14-22,7,8:1-14

Doris J. McMillan

TOWER OF BABEL

After the great flood, the earth was of one speech,
Men began to build a city and tower, they wanted heaven to reach;
The Lord came down to see what they had build
And knew that their imaginations would run while at will;
If one language was spoken by each.

God confused their languages and made it hard for them to unravel,
And because of this, the city was called Babel;
He scattered them all about
They went here, there, and without;
Upon the earth as they roamed in travel.

Genesis 11:1-9

SODOM AND GOMORRAH

Two wicked cities named Sodom and Gomorrah,
Destroyed by brimstone and fire, such horror!
As they went down in flames
Lot's wife looked back and became;
A pillar of salt, what sorrow, what sorrow!

Genesis 19:24-26

Doris J. McMillan

ABRAHAMS'S COVENANT

Sarai, old and childless, approached her husband Abram, and said,
"Go, in unto Hagar, so I may obtain children by my Eygptian handmaid;"
So a child was conceived by Hagar
Suggested by Abram's wife Sarai;
But this was not in the plan God had laid.

God spoke to Abram and said in his conversation,
"I will establish my covenant between me and thee," and to your generation;
The convenant between Abram and God was arranged
And following this, his name was changed;
To Abraham: "The father of many nations."

Hagar was despised by Sarai, and in the home there was friction,
So Hagar fled into the desert to escape her mistress' inflictions;
An angel of the Lord appeared before her to foretell
That her unborn son will be named Ishmael;
Because the Lord had heard her afflictions.

Sarai's name was also changed as God said it would be,
And that he would bless her with a son in her old age, indeed!
Her new name shall be called Sarah, "Mother of nations."
Kings shall come down through her generations;
With an everlasting covenant with Isaac, their son of Abraham's seed.

Genesis 16, 17

ABRAHAM'S TEST OF FAITH

God sent Abraham into the land of Moriah, and tempted him with this test,
To offer Isaac, his son, as burnt offerings upon a mountain, was the request;
Abraham obeyed God, took Isaac there, with wood, fire, and knife
Isaac asked: "Father, where is the lamb for the sacrifice?"
Upon the altar he laid and tied Isaac, to give God his very best.

Abraham lifted the knife over the altar and Isaac, as he lay,
An angel of the Lord called out, "harm not your son, neither shall you slay;
You have not withheld your son from me, and I know it is God that you fear."
Abraham looked back and saw a ram trapped in a bush very near;
He sacrificed it instead, and named the place Jehovah-Jireh, known to this day.

Genesis 22:1-14

Doris J. McMillan

ESAU AND JACOB

Isaac and Rebekah had two sons; Esau and Jacob by name,
Esau was red and hairy, Jacob was plain;
Jacob stayed in the tents of his home
Esau preferred the fields to hunt and roam;
But the parent's love for each son was not the same.

Isaac love Esau, a skillful hunter as a boy,
Rebekah loved Jacob who was shy and coy;
Esau hunted venison meat
Which his father Isaac loved to eat;
While Jacob made "red pottage;" cooking was his joy.

Esau came from hunting, hungry and weak,
He felt faint and everything looked bleak;
But before giving him food, Jacob made him swear
To sell him the "birthright" which Esau despised, and with despair;
Sold it to Jacob for something to drink, and food to eat.

Genesis 25:27-34

JACOB'S VISION OF A LADDER

In a certain place, Jacob made a pillow of stones to lay his head upon that night,
He dreamed of a ladder reaching from earth to heaven; it was of great height;
Envisioned on it, angels of God, who ascended and descended
Above it, the Lord God of Abraham and Isaac, stood suspended;
Jacob awoke and fearfully said, God's House, the gate of heaven is on this site.

The land on which Jacob slept, God promised to give it to his seed,
They will become as dust of the earth, plentiful and will succeed;
Spreading abroad from the north, south, east, and west
Through their generations, all families will be blest;
Then brought back into the land, which God gave them, the rightful deed.

Jacob set the stones which he had made for a pillow, in an upright position,
Poured oil on it, and named it Beth-el, previously known as Luz by definition;
Jacob vowed if God let him returned to his father's house in peace
All that God give to him, he will give back a tenth of his increase;
And the pillar of stones shall be God's house, a place of recognition.

Genesis 28:11-22

JACOB'S NAME CHANGED TO ISRAEL

Jacob wrestled with a man until the break of day was nigh,
He prevailed not against him, and touched the hollow of his thigh;
Jacob's thigh came out of its socket and disjointed
The man said, "let me go," Jacob refused, and directly pinpointed;
"I will not let you go until you bless me," his request, a priority high.

The man asked Jacob his name, and later changed it to Israel,
Then said, as a prince, you have power with God, men, and prevailed well;
The man blessed him, and Jacob said, I have observed
God face to face, and my life is preserved;
And Jacob called the name of the place where he wrestled, Peniel.

Genesis 32:24-31

JOSEPH SOLD INTO EGYPT

Long ago in the land of Canaan lived twelve brothers,
They had the same father, but different mothers;
Joseph, the youngest had a colorful coat
His jealous brothers dipped it in the blood of a goat;
And sold him, after conspiring with one another.

Joseph was carried by Ishmeelites into Egypt's land,
Where Potiphar, Pharoah's guard bought him off their hands;
Later Joseph was falsely accused by Potiphar's wife
Thrown into prison, which could have been for the rest of his life;
Instead was freed, and in Pharoah's house, became second in command.

Genesis 37

Doris J. McMillan

JOSEPH INTERPRETS THE DREAM

Jopseph was known as an interpreter of dreams by name,
This interpretation of Pharoah's dream was the beginning of his fame;
Seven lean cows came and ate seven fat cows, Joseph revealed to him
Seven food ears of grains sprang up, but seven thin ones ate them;
And urged Pharoah to gather food, before seven years of famine came.

Many countries came into Egypt to buy food during the famine,
Jacob sent ten of his sons, but kept at home, Benjamin;
The sons traveled Into Egypt for corn to buy
Approached Joseph, the Govenor, to purchase a supply;
Not recognizing their brother, but Joseph knew them.

Genesis 41

JOSEPH REVEALS HIMSELF TO BROTHERS

Joseph wanted to see Benjamin, his youngest brother,
They were born of Rachael, Jacob's second wife, their mother;
Jacob at first refused, but later let him go
When Joseph saw Benjamin, he yearned to let him know;
Who he was, and later revealed himself to all the others.

When Jacob knew that Joseph was alive,
He said: "I will go to see him before I die."
Joseph delivered his family from the famine's oppression
Gave them silver, clothes, food and many possessions;
And brought them out of Canaan, into the land of Goshen to reside.

Genesis 45-47

Doris J. McMillan

MOSES, THE BEGINNING

Pharoah charged that every Hebrew son be cast into the river's waters,
A Levi woman hid her son in an ark of bulrushes, by the river's borders;
The sister watched from a distance to see what would happen to the child
Pharoah's daughter who came to bathe, saw the ark from the river's side;
Sent her maids to retrieve it, and they brought the ark to her upon her orders.

The sister requested to select a Hebrew nurse, from among the others,
It was granted, and she brought a woman to nurse her baby brother;
Pharoah's daughter said to woman: "Take this child away
And nurse it for me, and I will give thee thy wages," as pay;
The woman nursed here own son, for the sister brought in the child's mother.

Pharoah's daughter named him Moses, because "out of the water," he was drawn,
Became her son, but later went among his own people, when he was grown
He saw and Egyptian beat a Hebrew brethren one day
Killed the Egyptian, when no one was looking his way;
Then fled for his life from Pharoah's face when his deed was known.

Exodus 2:1-14

MOSES AND THE BURNING BUSH

An angel appeared to Moses in the midst of a bush engulfed with fire,
The bush burned, but was not consumed, as the blazes rose higher;
God called to Moses out of the flame
"Moses, Moses." When he answered his name;
God instructed him to take off his shoes, as he came closer to inquire.

God said, the ground where you stand is a holy place,
Identified himself to Moses who was afraid to look upon his face;
Said to Moses, I have seen my people in Egypt, and their afflictions;
They, will I deliver into a land of milk and honey, rich with my grace.

The Egyptians oppressed them greatly, and God heard their lamentations,
Chose Moses to send unto Pharoah, to request his people's liberations
God revealed his name unto Moses boldly, "I AM THAT I AM"
Tell the children of Israel who sent you, and memorialize this monogram;
"I AM, the God of Abraham, Isaac, and Jacob, my name to all generations."

Exodus 3:1-15

Doris J. McMillan

MOSES AND THE RED SEA

Moses led his people through the wilderness out of the Eygptians' hand,
Pharoah chased them to the Red Sea with his army of host and band;
When Moses stretched out his hand as the Lord guided
Over the Red Sea, the waters miracously divided;
And the Israelites walked in its midst on dry land.

Now Pharoah tried to be bold and brave,
Has his army to follow Israelites by orders he gave;
But a strange phenonmenon occurred
The Red Sea waters returned as they were;
Covering all of Pharoah's army, and no one was saved.

Exodus 14

JOSHUA

The Lord spoke to Joshua, son of Nun, and gave him a hugh task,
When told to carry on after Moses had died, he had no questions to ask;
The Lord said, "To you and all the people I will give the land
And before thee, there shall not any man be able to stand;
As I was with Moses, I will be with them." His words wear no mask.

Then Joshua sent two men as spies into the country, high and low,
To view and seek out the land, and also the city of Jericho;
They secretly left for the countryside to evade and to dodge
The enemy, until they came to a harlot's house to lodge;
When the king of Jericho asked where the men were, she said, "I do not know."

This harlot who lived in Jericho was named Rahab,
She had a reputation, which was considered bad;
Hid the spies of Joshua until it was safe and clear
And said, "We have heard of your God, and Him we fear;
Save my family!" They promised to do so, and this made her glad.

Now the city of Jericho was tightly sealed, secured and fast,
Joshua marched around the city six days, and blew a ram's horn with a blast;
At the sound of the trumpet, the people began to shout
As they continued to go around and about;
The walls of Jericho weakened and fell flat; they could not last.

Joshua 1:1-8, 2:1-14, 6:1-5

Doris J. McMillan

DEBORAH AND BARAK

When Israel was judged by Deborah, the prophetess,
The children of Israel came to her, for their cause to address;
She told Barak to take with him ten thousand men to stand
Against Sisera, whom the Lord will deliver into Barak's hand;
For the children of Israel under Jabin's captivity, were greatly oppressed.

Barak said to Deborah, I will go only if you go along,
But if you will not go, I will stay here where I belong;
Deborah agreed to go, but not for his esteem to travel abroad
But her journey with him will be only to honor the Lord;
And after Sisera's defeat and death, Deborah sang her victory song.

Judges 4:4-9

GIDEON

When the Israelites did evil in the Lord's sight,
God chose Gideon, a man of valour and might;
To save Israel out of the Midianites' hands
With the Lord's help he would take a stand;
For he had found grace it the Lord's sight.

Gideon took three hundred men to fight,
They surrounded and attacked the enemy at night;
Blew trumpets on every side of the camp
With the Lord's sword in one hand, and in the other, a lamp;
Conquered the enemy, and saved Israel from the Midianites.

Judges 6:11-17, 7:16-25

Doris J. McMillan

SAMSON

Samson was a man of great strength,
The source of it came from his hair long in length;
But when he gave his secret away
To an enticing woman named Delilah that day;
Into the Philistines' hands he went.

The Philistines shaved his hair and put out his eyes,
Securely bound him with brass chains and ties;
Overtime his hair began to grow
Praying daily to God his strength to restore;
While his enemies ridiculed and displayed him as their prize.

Samson asked God to remember him, and did not doubt,
And to avenge his enemies who put his eyes out;
Took hold of two pillars, each on his left and right
Brought down the house with all his might;
Upon himself and all the Philistines about.

Judges 16:5-30

RUTH AND NAOMI

When Ruth's husband died, Noami, the mother-in-law said,
Return to your country of Moab, to obtain food and bread;
Ruth refused to go back and serve heathen gods
Preferred to stay with Naomi and lodge;
Accepted her people, and the God of Israel instead.

Ruth said to Naomi: "Whither thou goest, I will go,
Whither thou lodgest, I will lodge also;
Your people and your God will be mine, she replied
And where you are buried, I will be buried there when I die;"
Naomi saw Ruth was persistent, and did not speak of her leaving anymore.

Ruth 1:1-16

Doris J. McMillan

ISRAEL REQUESTS A KING

Joel and Abiah, the first and second sons of Samuel,
Were appointed by him to judge over Israel;
His sons decided to go their own ways, and did abstain
From walking as Samuel did, for their own monetary gains;
Taking bribes, and perverting judgement, as they rebelled.

The elders of Israel came to Samuel in congregations,
Requested to have a king to judge them, like other nations;
Samuel was displeased, and went unto the Lord to pray
The Lord told him to listen to what they had to say;
But they rejected Samuel, and also the Lord with indignations.

The Lord told Samuel to show what manner of king over them, shall reign,
Let them see all the inflictions upon their sons and daughters, he shall bring;
The people refused to listen to Samuel's voice
Preferred to have a king over them, as choice;
Then the Lord said, "listen to what they say, and make them a king."

1 Samuel 8:1-22

HANNAH, MOTHER OF SAMUEL

Hannah had no children; she grieved bitterly and longed,
While praying to the Lord for a child of her own;
She vowed: "Lord if you will give a male child to your handmaid
I will give him to you all of his life, and no razor shall come upon his head."
She conceived, and named him Samuel, when he was born.

! Samuel 1:1-19

DAVID ANNOINTED KING

The Lord sent his servant Samuel,
To Jesse's house to find a king for Israel;
And to anoint him with a horn of oil
For the Lord had rejected king Saul;
Who had disobeyed the Lord God and rebelled.

Seven of Jesse's sons were presented, but not selected,
Then came David who was godly looking and respected;
He was Jesse's youngest son
And Samuel anointed him as the one;
Whom the Lord had chosen as His elected.

1 Samuel 16:1-13

DAVID AND GOLIATH

Now David was a brave shepherd boy,
Who used a sling of stones as a weapon, not a toy;
To kill a Philistine giant
Who was boastful and defiant;
On that day, the children of Israel shouted for joy.

When Goliath, the giant fell to the ground dead,
David took the giant's sword and cut off his head;
After the courage of David was displayed
And victory brought to the Israelites that day;
With no champion to defend them, the Philistines turned and fled.

Samuel 17:49-51

Doris J. McMillan

SOLOMON

Solomon was chosen by God to build a great temple,
A task that was not so plain and simple,
He did not need an outline
God gave him the design;
And he began it to God's plan without a whimple.

The walls and floors were covered with cedar wood, a sight to behold,
Ornamented in precious stones and overlaid in gold;
When he completed the beautiful edification
He brought into it sacred things and gave a dedication;
To place in the house of the Lord, as promised by God and foretold.

When the Queen of Sheba heard of Solomon's glory and fame,
She came to Jerusalem bringing spices and gold on her camel train;
After seeing all of his prosperity and wisdom
And presenting gifts for his kingdom;
She left for the country from which she came.

1 Kings 6,7,8,10

DIVIDED HOUSES

When Israel heard that Jeroboam had come again,
He was sent to the congregation, and make him king within;
Some followed Jeroboam, whose desire to rule Israel was avid
Only the tribe of Judah followed the house of David;
Then Rehoboam came, and assembled it with the tribe of Benjamin.

Rehoboam chose several thousand men to fight the house of Israel with stern,
Shemaiah was sent by God to Rehoboam, and the house of Judah with concern;
To tell them not to go up against one another
Nor to fight the children of Israel, their brother;
They listened, and every man returned to his house, with no discern.

1 Kings 12:20-24

Doris J. McMillan

JEROBOAM'S IDOLS

Jeroboam built two cities, Shechem and Penuel, and said silently in his heart,
The kingdom shall now return to the house of David, and no longer be apart;
If by chance, the people return to their lord, they will have me killed
And will go again to Rehoboam, king of Judah of their own will;
Thinking the worst, he devised a plan, so they would not depart.

After consulting with others, and making two calves of gold,
He said to Israel, it is too much for you to go into Jerusalem, Behold!
These are the gods which brought you out of Egypt's land
Then he set up one idol in Beth-el, and the other in Dan;
Made priests of the lowest people, not the sons of Levi, as of old.

A certain month in Beth-el, he ordained, and imitated Judah's feast,
Sacrificed unto his callves, and of high places, selected priests;
Established and decreed by order, his own feast in Beth-el,
A place of worship upon the alter, for the children of Israel;
Where he made offerings and burned incense to the golden beast.

1 Kings 12:25-33

ELIJAH MEETS THE WIDOW WOMAN

The Lord commanded Elijah to go to a place and reside,
In the home of a widow woman, where he was to abide;
When he arrive in the city
He saw a poor widow woman of pity;
Gathering sticks to make a cooking fire.

"Bring me a vessel of water, then a small piece of bread," he confided,
"I have but a handful of meal and a jar of oil," she replied;
"Look I am gathering two sticks," she said and revealed
"To prepare the last of this oil and meal;
So that my son and I may eat it and die."

Elijah told her to not be afraid, but to go and do as he say,
Make a cake for him first; then told her, without delay;
The Lord God of Israel said the meal and oil would not run out
She went and did exactly what Elijah said, and did not doubt;
And the woman, her son and Elijah had food for many days.

1Kings 17:1-16

Doris J. McMillan

ELIJAH HEALS THE WIDOW'S SON

One day, the widow's son fell deathly ill,
The child became breathless, lifeless and still;
She ask of Elijah, for what purpose had he come
To remind her of her sin, or to kill her son?
Elijah carried the child to his bed, in an upper room where he lived.

Elijah asked God, had he brought evil upon the widow's roof?
He prayed to the Lord to let the child live again; then had the proof;
His prayers were answered when breath came into the child
When he gave the child to his mother, revived and alive;
The widow knew Elijah was a man of God, who spoke the truth.

1Kings 17:17-24

NABOTH'S VINEYARD

Naboth, the Jezreelite's, inherited from his fathers, a vineyard,
It was near the palace of King Ahab who pressed Naboth for it hard.
Ahab said, "give me your vineyard for my garden of herbs, if you may
I will give you a better vineyard than you have now, or what it is worth in pay;"
When Naboth refused, Ahab became sad, refused to eat, and lost self-regard.

Jezebel saw her husband's rejection and depression, then proposed an appeal,
To get Naboth's vineyard, she wrote letters, and signed them with Ahab's seal;
Sent them to the elders and nobles where Naboth live, to proclaimed a fast
To have Naboth brought before the people and tried as an outcast;
Then appointed two men as witnesses, with whom she had made a crooked deal.

When the men of Naboth's city read the letters Jezebel wrote, they complied,
After the two men she sent, witnessed against Naboth, and falsely testified;
Then they set Naboth high among the people, and charged with an evil thing
Saying in the presence of them, he had blasphemed God and the king;
Then they carried Naboth out of the city, and stoned him until he died.

1 Kings 21:1-14

JEZEBEL AND KING AHAB

Jezebel, a wicked and evil pagan queen,
Persecuted the prophets; she was cruel, sinful and mean;
Dogs ate her flesh when she died
As Elijah had prophesied;
And brought an end to her vicious, conniving schemes.

Ahab, king of Israel, and husband of Jezebel,
Was a thief and murderer, and equally evil as well;
Elijah foretold an event following his death would incur
Dogs would lick his blood, and this did occur;
As blood was washed from his chariot, where he mortally fell.

1 Kings 19-1;22:23

NAAMAN HEALED FROM LEPROSY

The Syrians captured and carried away a little Israelite maid,
She waited on Naaman's wife, to whom she approached and said;
My lord would recover if he were with the prophet in Samaria
Then one who heard the maid, reported it to the king of Syria;
Who sent a letter to Israel's king by Naaman with gold and silver to be paid.

The letter was brought to the king, and its contents revealed,
Naaman was sent to be cleansed of Leprosy and to be healed;
The king believed this was an attempt to incite an argument, and was outraged
He began to tear his clothing and asked, "Am I God?" He was enraged;
Then Elisha sent word to the king, "let Naaman come to me now." He urgently appealed.

Naaman arrived by horses and chariot at Elisha's house, and stood at the door,
Elisha sent him a message, "Go wash in the Jordan seven times and be restored;"
Naaman angrily said, "I thought Elisha would come out and take a stand
Call on his lord, and heal my leprosy by striking it with his hand;
Are not the Rivers of Damascus better than Israel's waters?" He implored.

His servants asked, "If the prophet told you to do something great, would you not endure?
How much rather then, when he says, Wash and be clean, to receive a cure?"
Naaman dipped in the Jordan seven times as the man of God implied
The leprosy disappeared, and his flesh reappeared as that of a little child;
Now Naaman recognized Elisha as a man of God, for making him clean and pure.

2 Kings 5:1-14

Doris J. McMillan

REBUILDING THE TEMPLE

The Jewish elders who were brave and bold,
Rebuilded the temple, and prospered through prophets of old;
Not by the decrees of three Persian Kings' fling
But by the commandment of God, Israel's King
Completed and dedicated the house of God as they were told.

Ezra 6:14-16

NEHEMIAH

The king's cupbearer named Nehemiah,
Approached the king with a request and a desire;
To rebuild Jerusalem's wall
That will stand great and tall;
To protect the city that God admired.

Nehemiah went alone in the night with a plan,
To view the broken walls of Jerusalem, his father's land;
When he saw the gates burned and city in waste
He returned and said: "Let us build and no longer be a disgrace;
For I am under the goodness of God's hand."

So Nehemiah with his chosen men repaired the wall,
For God had answered his prayers, fastings and calls;
Each man did his portion of repair and part
Worked diligently in spirit, mind, and heart;
Then joined the wall together all in all.

Nehemiah 1-4

Doris J. McMillan

ESTHER AND MORDECAI

Esther was a beautiful young Jewish maid,
Raised by her uncle Mordecai, for her parents were dead;
She was brought before the king's sight
He loved her above all, and being pleased with delight;
Made her queen and placed a crown on her head.

The king promoted Haman above all the princes,
The king's servants bowed to him and paid reverences;
He commanded Mordecai to bow
When he would not, Haman vowed;
To destroy all the Jews throughout the provinces.

Now Haman was a very wicked man,
He plotted against Mordecai with an evil plan;
Esther, the queen exposed him before the king's face
The king condenmed Haman to death, and to take the place;
On the same gallows he'd prepared for Mordecai to hang.

Esther Chapter 2-7

JOB'S TEST: POSSESSIONS LOST

In the land of Uz, there lived a perfect and upright man,
Named Job, who feared God, and avoided evil at every stand;
One day Satan came to God and asked to put Job to a test
God knew that Job was his servant of integrity, one of the best;
Gave permission, but kept Job's life in His hand.

Satan presented God with several propositions,
That Job would curse him to his face, if attacked with afflictions;
He lost his children, cattle and all he had
Then his skin became covered with boils that looked bad;
But he did not sin against God, and Satan lost in his predictions.

Job's wife said to him: "Curse God and die."
But Job did not sin with his lips, in God he trusted and relied;
Instead, he cursed the day he was born
And for darkness to come upon that day, and let it not be joined;
To the days of the year, nor to the number of months be applied.

Job 1,2,3:1-6

Doris J. McMillan

JOB'S FAITH: POSSESSIONS RESTORED

Job remained faithful, and God did restore,
Twice as much as he had before;
He gave him three fair daughters, and seven sons
Then livestock were increased by the thousands;
In the end, Job was blessed greater than in the beginning, with much more.

Job lived a hundred and forty years,
He was able to see four generations of his sons' sons reared;
Job lived a full life, and died being very old
But the story of his faithfulness will forever be told;
Of a man who humbled himself to the God he revered.

Job 42:12-17

THE SECRET PLACE OF GOD

When we dwell in the secret place of the most High,
We live safely under His shadow, not a whisper or sigh;
God will deliver us from harm
As He covers us with the wings of His arms;
And shields us with His truth, which is always nigh.

Our enemies we can overcome and beat,
We can trample over them with our feet;
The Holy angels will take charge and stand
To protect us from evil, at God's command;
And with His salvation, we will conquer and defeat.

Psalms 91

Doris J. McMillan

ISAIAH'S VISION OF THE LORD

In the year King Uzziah died, Isaiah saw the Lord sitting upon a throne,
High and lifted up, his great robe covered and filled the temple alone;
Above it seraphims with six wings, two covered his face, feet, and with two did fly
One voice shouted to another," Holy, Holy, Holy, is the Lord of hosts," was the cry;
"The whole earth is full of his glory," and the door posts moved at his voice and tone.

Isaiah said, "I have unclean lips and live among people likewise, unworthy to be,
In the presence of the King, the Lord of Host; my eyes have no right to see;"
Then one of the seraphim took a live coal in a tong, flew up and with a surge
Laid it upon Isaiah's mouth and said, "thy iniquity is taken away, thy sin is purged."
The Lord asked, "Whom shall I send to go for us," Isaiah said, "here am I, send me."

Isaiah 6:1-8

BROKEN CLAY BOTTLE

The Lord told Jeremiah to get a potter's clay bottle, take the elders and the priests,
Then go into the valley of Hinnom's son, near the entrance of the gate on the east;
There proclaim these words to the King of Judah, and the people of Jerusalem
The Lord will bring evil upon this place, with emptiness, death, and mayhem;
He will make this city desolate, and give your bodies as meat for the beasts.

They have forsaken me, estranged the place, and burned incense,
Unto foreign gods, and filled it with the blood of innoncents;
You shall break the bottle in the sight of the men that go along, and say
The Lord will break the people, and this city, as one breaks a jar of clay;
And will bury them, until there is no place to bury in Tophet, are his intents.

Jeremiah 19

Doris J. McMillan

BESIEGE OF JERUSALEM

King Zedekiah knew that Nebuchadnezzar was set against Jerusalem for war,
He inquired Jeremiah's help from the Lord to have the Babylonian king withdraw;
Jeremiah said, the Lord refuses to help, but will give the people ways to decide,
Choose the way of life and survive, or choose the way of death and die;
Because the Lord was angry with them for their sins, and breaking his law.

He that stay in the city, shall die by the sword, famine, and disease,
But He that surrenders, shall live, and his life, shall the Chaldeans seize;
The Lord has set his face against Jerusalem for evil, and it will not stand
The Chaldeans shall invade the city, and it shall fall into their hands;
And Jerusalem shall be burned by fire, in the Babylonian besiege.

Jeremiah 21:1-10

EZEKIEL

God gave Ezekiel a commission,
To tell the House of Israel concerning their sinful condition;
Whether they will take heed and hear
Or whether they will forebear;
They will know a prophet had been sent to them with a mission.

God warned Ezekiel not to be afraid that briers and scorpions dwell about,
Not be rebellious, but to eat what He gives, and to open his mouth;
And then suddenly Ezekiel looked
He saw a hand, and a roll of a book;
Where weeping, mourning, and woes were written, within and without.

Ezekiel 2

Doris J. McMillan

VALLEY OF DRY BONES

Ezekiel was carried out by the hand and Spirit of the Lord, and set down alone,
In the middle of a valley, which was full of dry bones;
The Lord had him to passed by them around and about
There witnessed many bones lying dried up, within and without;
The Lord ask, "Can these bones live again?" Ezekiel said "thou knowest," in a positive tone.

The Lord told Ezekiel, prophesy to these bones so they may hear,
He spoke to them, and made the words of the Lord clear;
That they will have a body, covered with skin, and given breath
They shall know the Lord restored them to life from death;
This he prophesied, as the Lord commanded without fear.

I prophesied, then there was a noise; bones to bones began to meet,
They lived, and a great, superior army of men stood upon their feet;
These are the whole house of Israel, cut off from its parts
Prophesy, the Lord will bring them out of their graves, with a new start;
Into the land of Israel, to once again be together and complete.

Ezekeiel 37:1-12

MESCHACH, SHADRACH & ABEDNEGO

There once lived three young Jewish men,
Thrown in a furnace of fire when they would not sin;
For refusing to bow down as told
To worship the king's image of gold;
But their God delivered them from a fiery end.

In the furnace King Nebuchadnezzar saw something odd,
Shook his head, asked in amazement and nodded;
"Did we not throw in three?
But now a fourth one I see;
And it looks like the Son of God."

Daniel 3:8-25

Doris J. McMillan

DANIEL INTERPRETS THE KING'S DREAM

In Babylon lived a king who had strange dreams,
But did not know what they meant so it seems;
Daniel interpreted these things
To Nebuchadnezzar the king,
That his life would not be one of peaches and cream.

Nebuchadnezzar dwelled with the beasts of the fields,
With the oxen, grass became his meal;
At the end of his days
He changed his ways;
And honored the King of Heaven with his seal.

Daniel 4

DANIEL INTERPRETS THE HANDWRITING ON THE WALL

Belshazzar the king gave a feast with plenty wine,
Used the temple's vessels to serve his princes, wives, and concubines;
Suddenly, fingers of a hand began writing on a wall
The frightened king shouted loudly with a call;
"A third of my kingdom I will give to anyone who interprets the sign."

Daniel was brought before Belshazzar the king,
He said, I will interpret it, but keep your gifts, I do not want a thing,
The writing says, God has numbered your kingdom and has decided
That your kingdom is finished and divided;
On that same night, Belshazzar the king was slain.

Daniel 5 & 6

Doris J. McMillan

DANIEL IN THE LIONS' DEN

Darius became king and established a decree,
That anyone who prays to other gods, or fall upon his knees;
Would be punished for not honoring the compliance
And casted into a den of lions for defiance;
Because this was the law, according to the Medes.

So Daniel was thrown into the lions' den,
For charges brought against him by the king's men;
God sent an angel to shut the lions' mouths
And delivered Daniel without;
A scratch on his body or skin.

Daniel 6

JONAH

Jonah fled from the Lord's presence to reach,
A place called Tarshish, instead of Ninevah to preach;
He boarded a ship with a fearful crew
Who offered a sacrifice to the Lord, so they threw;
Jonah into the sea, not on the beach.

The Lord had a great fish to come along,
To swallow up Jonah who had done wrong;
Three days and nights in its belly he stayed
The Lord amswered him when he prayed;
And Jonah came out to dry land where he belonged.

Jonah 1 & 2

Doris J. McMillan

TITHES AND OFFERINGS

Bring me all the tithes and offerings, God employed,
That there will be meat in my house for you to enjoy;
Prove me to my word and believe
I will give you more blessings than you will be able to receive;
And protect you from the devourer that comes to destroy.

Malachi 3:10-11

THE NEW TESTAMENT

Doris J. McMillan

BIRTH OF JESUS

Mary, a young Jewish virgin girl,
Owned neither money nor jewerly with pearls;
She was favored above all others
Chosen by God to be the mother;
Of Jesus, the Savior of the world.

Joseph, engaged to Mary, had a plan to spare her from public rejection,
But an angel appeared to him in a dream and explained the conception;
He was told a son shall be born unto Mary
Jesus and Emmanuel, are names he will carry;
And he shall save his people from sins' infection.

Matthew 1:18-25
Luke 1:27-33

Doris J. McMillan

SHEPHERDS TOLD OF JESUS' BIRTH

In Bethlehem one night, shepherds watched over their flock on one accord,
Suddenly in shining glory, there appeared before them, an angel of the Lord;
Saying, "do not be afraid, look, I bring you good tidings of great joy
Which shall be for all people to enjoy;
Because a Saviour is born in the city of David, which is Christ the Lord."

The angel gave a sign where to find the baby Jesus, and said unto them,
He will be wrapped in swaddling clothes, lying in a manger in Bethlehem;
Suddenly, tribute and honor to God that night was paid
As the angel and heavenly host, shouted praises, said;
Glory to God in the highest, peace on earth, good will toward men.

Luke 2:8-14

WISE MEN FOLLOW THE STAR TO BETHLEHEM

When Jesus was born in Bethlehem's Judea of a special birth,
Wise men guided by a star to Jerusalem, traveled from the eastern part of the earth;
When they found the child in Bethlehem, they fell down and worshipped him in reverence
Laid opened treasures before the child in his mother's presence;
Their gifts of gold, frankincense and myrrh.

Herod sent the wise men to find the place where Jesus was born
And to return to him with word, so he may also go to worship and adorn;
In a dream, the wise men were warned by God of Herod's scheme
Not to go back and report to Herod what they had seen;
So they left Jerusalem, and departed into the country of their own.

Matthew 2:1-12

Doris J. McMillan

JOHN THE BAPTIST

John the Baptist preached in the wilderness of Judea,
People came from all regions to hear;
He said that someone was coming mightier and higher
Who would baptize them with the Holy Ghost and fire;
And whose shoes he was not worthy to bear.

When John baptized Jesus, the heavens opened above,
The spirit of God descended upon Him like a dove;
A voice loudly acclaimed
Well pleased! God proclaimed;
With Jesus, His Son whom He loved.

ST. Matthew 3:1-17

JESUS TEMPTED BY THE DEVIL

Jesus was led by the Spirit into the wilderness,
To be tempted by the devil who was filled with bitterness;
He fasted forty days and nights
With nothing to eat in sight;
But He was filled with the Spirit of Righteousness.

The devil tempted Jesus when He was hungry and weak,
With miracles to perform and world kingdoms at his feet;
Jesus quoted the written words each time that day
And chased the devil with the Holy Scriptures away;
Then Satan left and went away in defeat.

Matthew 4:1-9

Doris J. McMillan

MAN WITH UNCLEAN SPIRIT

Jesus entered into the synagogue on the Sabbath Day;
He taught with authority, and surprised others with what he had to say;
A man with an unclean spirit cried out
"Jesus of Nazareth, the Holy One, I know you, and what you are all about;
You will destroy us and send us away."

"Hold thy peace, and come out of him," was Jesus' command,
Shaking and crying loudly, the evil spirit came out of the man;
The people looked at each other, and began to convey
"What is this new teaching that unclean spirits obey?"
They were amazed and did not understand.

Mark 1:23-27

JESUS, THE POWERFUL HEALER

Many people were brought to Jesus, whose bodies were diseased,
Those with unclean spirits, bound, tormented and displeased;
The sick, the lame, the devil-possessed
A leper who came kneeling and begging, with a cleansing request;
Jesus healed them all, and put their sicknesses at ease.

Mark 1:34-42

Doris J. McMillan

PARALYZED MAN

Four people carried a man who was paralyzed,
To a place where Jesus was, but it was impossible to get inside;
So they lowered him through the roof
Jesus said, "Son, thy sins be forgiven," for their faith was proof;
But the scribes who heard Jesus began to criticize.

Jesus knew within the Scribes minds evil stalked,
Full of disbelief and blasphemous talk;
But Jesus asked them, "What is easier to say?"
To the paralyzed man who lay;
"Arise, take up thy bed and walk?"

He said to the man, "But that you may know,
That the Son for Man has power on earth to forgive sins," and do more;
"Arise, take up thy bed and go to your home;"
Immediately the man arose and went on his own
And all were astonished; they had never seen anything like this before.

Mark 2:1-12

MAN WITH THE WITHERED HAND

On the Sabbath Day in the synagogue, Jesus saw a man,
Who had a crippled and dried up hand;
The people watched closely to accuse him at will
But Jesus asked: "Which is right, to do good or evil, to save a life or to kill?"
Then the man stretched out his hand, and it was healed on Jesus' command.

Mark 3:1-5

Doris J. McMillan

PARABLE OF THE SOWER

Jesus taught many people the parable: "Sower of Seeds,"
When sown, some were devoured, scorched, and choked with weeds;
While some fell on good ground
And yield and abundance of fruit all around;
As he taught the parable, he urged the people to listen and take heed.

When the seed is planted, it grows during the night or daylight.
Whether the sower is awake or asleep at night;
Without any help the seed continues to grow
How? The man does not know;
And the fruit is harvested when the time is right.

Jesus compared the kingdom of God to a seed in the ground,
A grain of mustard seed, so tiny and round;
Although it is very small
Among the herbs, it grows greater than all;
Because the seed that was sown remained faithful, steady, and sound.

Mark 4:1-9, 30-34

MAN WITH A LEGION OF DEVILS

Jesus came into the country of Gadarenes one day,
Inside the body of a man living there, a Legion of devils lay;
When Jesus cast them out into a herd of swine
They ran violently, and choked in a sea of brine;
The man departed, telling others of his healing along the way.

Mark 5:1-20

Doris J. McMillan

JARIUS' DAUGHTER

Many people waited on the seashore for Jesus, to meet and to greet,
A synagogue ruler named Jarius saw him and fell at his feet;
"My little girl lay near death", he said, and made an appeal
"Come lay hands on her that she may be healed;"
Jesus went with him when he heard the man's urgent entreat.

While they were talking the ruler was told his daughter lay dead,
Jesus said, "Only believe and do not be afraid,"
He did not let the crowd follow along
But instead took with him Peter, James and John;
To the ruler's house, where he saw people crying around the little girl's bed.

Jesus asked them, "Why are you making much of this and weeping?
She is not dead, but only sleeping;"
When the people laugh with doubt
Jesus put all of them out;
Then entered the room with the girl's parents, and started the proceedings.

Jesus took the twelve year old girl's hand and said arise,
She sat up straight to everyone's surprise;
When she arose to her feet
He said give her something to eat;
And commanded that no man know of this, or made wise.

Mark 5:21-23, 35-43

WOMAN SICK FOR TWELVE YEARS

A woman with an issue of blood for twelve years,
Touched Jesus as he was passing near;
She knew if she touched his clothes
She would be made whole;
And immediately her blood dried up, and her disease disappeared.

Jesus turned and asked: "Who touched me?'
His disciples said, "you ask this, when many are pressing against thee;"
The fearful woman fell down trembling and revealed
That it was she who touched him and was healed;
He said: "Your faith have made you whole, go in peace and be plague free."

Mark 5:25-34

Doris J. McMillan

DEAF AND DUMB MAN

A man who could not hear or clearly speak his name,
Was brought to Jesus because of his healing fame;
When Jesus spoke to and touched the man's tongue and ears
The man was healed, able to talk and to hear;
With opened ears and loosened tongue, he was never again the same.

Mark 7:32-35

GREATEST APOSTLE

Jesus asked his disciples the reason for their dispute along the way,
They did not answer him; they had nothing to say;
For they argued who would be the greatest among themselves
But Jesus sat down and called together the twelve;
And to show them how to receive others, he used a child for his display.

James and John wanted Jesus to grant them a special command,
To sit in glory with him on the right or left hand;
Jesus answered them: "Are you aware of what you ask me to do?
Can you drink of the same cup and of the baptism too?
This you shall do, but it is not mine to give, but the Father's to those in His plan."

When the other disciples heard of it they were appalled,
But Jesus called them together and explained to all;
That among you whosoever will be great, your minister He shall be
And the one who is chief, shall be servant of all; for you see;
The Son of man came not to be ministered unto, but to give life to the great and small.

Mark 9:33-37, 10:35-45

Doris J. McMillan

RICH YOUNG MAN

There was a young man who had great possessions,
He wanted eternal life, but being rich became an obsession;
When Jesus told him to sell all he had
The man went away sad;
With a sorrowful and grieved expression.

Mark 10:17-22
Matthew 19:16-22

JESUS' RIDE INTO JERUSALEM

Jesus sent two disciples to a village nearby,
Where they were to find an unridden colt tied;
He told them to loose it and bring it to him
And if any man asks Why? Say unto him, or unto them;
That the Lord has need of it, and bring it over to this side.

The disciples found the colt tied at the door,
And began releasing it, but not before;
A certain of them asked, "What are you doing?' They demanded!
And when they were told this was what Jesus commanded;
They untied the colt and let it go.

They brought the colt to Jesus from abroad,
When he sat upon it and rode through the street, people applauded;
They threw down tree branches to show praises
Followed him and cried out chanting phrases;
"Hosanna! Blessed is He that come in the name of the Lord."

Mark 11:1-9

Doris J. McMillan

JESUS IN THE TEMPLE

Jesus cast out of the temple, those who bought and sold,
Turned over the moneychanger's tables, and asked with a scold;
"Is it not written, My house shall be called a house of prayer for all nations?
But you have made it a den of thieves." Their actions were desecrations;
Then the scribes and preists conspired to kill him, as their fears unfolded.

Mark 11:15-18

POOR WIDOW WOMAN

To the temple came a widow woman who was poor,
She threw in two mites, she had nothing more;
Jesus said she had done more than the rest
Because she had given her very best;
Than the rich who cast money into the treasury before.

Mark 12:42-44
Luke 21:2-3

Doris J. McMillan

SIGNS OF CHRIST'S COMING

A disciple made a remark about the temple's construction,
Jesus answered and prophesied of its destruction;
That the great buildings they see, will be thrown down, stone upon stone
Then four disciples who wanted to know more, asked him alone;
For a sign concerning the end times, he gave these instructions.

Jesus warned them; men will come in His name and deceive,
Saying, I am Christ, and by many, they shall be received;
When you hear of wars, do not be troubled or alarmed with fright
This is not the end, but after the tribulation, the sun nor moon shall give light;
And the stars shall fall, and the powers of heaven shall be shaken, Indeed!

Then the Son of Man with great power and glory shall appear,
And they shall see Him coming in the clouds, bright and clear;
The angels on a mission, He will send
To gather His elect from the four winds;
From the uutermost parts of earth and heaven, far and near.

That day or hour of the end, no man has this insight,
Not the angels, neither the Son, only the Father has this right;
Since you do not know the time, take heed; be ready, watch and pray
For the Son of Man, as the man who left his servants in charge while away;
May come at any time, whether it be at early morning, evening, or midnight.

Mark 13:1-7, 24-35

ELISABETH, MOTHER OF JOHN THE BAPTIST

Elisabeth was barren and also up in years of age,
The angel Gabriel appeared to Zacharias, her husband with a message;
That his wife was to bare a son named John
In the Lord he will be great and strong;
And will prepare the way for the Lord's earthly passage.

Luke 1:7-1

Doris J. McMillan

THE GOOD SAMARITAN

A man was attacked by thieves and left for dead,
They beat him, took his clothes and fled;
A priest and a Levite pass the man in need
But the Samaritan stopped and offered his good deed;
Cleaned and wrapped his wounds that bled.

The Samaritan took the man to an inn,
Where he proceded to take care of him;
Told the innkeeper as he began on his way
If his care costs more, I will repay;
When I return to your place again.

Luke 10:30-35

MARY AND MARTHA

Jesus was received into Martha's home,
Mary her sister was there, both whom he had known;
Martha had so much food to serve
And became disturbed;
Because she had to do the serving alone.

Martha asked Jesus, "Master do you not care,
That my sister has left the food for me to prepare?"
But Mary sat at Jesus' feet so near
For it was His words she wanted to hear;
And the differences in their ways, Jesus was much aware.

Jesus knew that Martha was careful and troubled at heart,
When she asked Him to bid Mary to help her, by giving His impart;
Jesus did not interfer with their duties, but gave Mary praise
Of a trait which will remain with her forever, He spoke this phrase;
"But one thing is needful, and Mary has chosen that good part."

Luke 10:38-42

Doris J. McMillan

THE TEN LEPER MEN

Jesus went to a certain village, and there within,
He met a group of ten leper men;
While standing far off and away
They lifted up their voices to say;
For Jesus, the Master to have mercy on them.

Jesus said, "Go show yourselves to the priests," and by His design,
They went and were cleansed, by His healing words of divine;
One of the lepers, a Samaritan, turned back after he was healed
Fell at Jesus' feet, gave thanks and glorified God, his gratitude revealed;
Then Jesus said, "Were there not ten cleansed? But where are the nine?"

Luke 17:12-19

BOASTFUL RICH MAN

A rich man with many goods to store,
Boasted to tear down his barns and build more;
But God told him that night he would die
And the treasures on which he relied;
Now to whom would they be left to adore?

Luke 12: 16-20

Doris J. McMillan

THE PRODIGAL SON

A certain man who had two sons,
Divided an inheritance when demanded by the younger one;
Who left his country and traveled far away
And did not save his money for a rainy day;
But instead wasted it living wildly, and having fun.

Later on, there was a famine in the land,
And his needs for food and money were much in demand;
He looked for work and did find
A job feeding, and later eating with swine;
While living in shame as a man's hired hand.

His situation was more than he could bear,
He knew his father had servants and enough food to spare;
Came to himself, and went to his father for repentance
Who forgave him, and with generous acceptances;
Clothed him in the best, honored him with a feast and fanfare.

The elder son heard music and dancing at the house, and learned,
That a celebration was being given for his brother who had returned;
Angrily wanted to know why a feast with a fatted calf
Was given in a rebellious son's behalf;
While never receiving anything for the time and work he had earned.

The father said, "All I have is yours, for you have always been around,
And now that I have received your brother home safely and sound;
Let us be happy that he is revived
For my son who was dead is alive;
Was lost, and now is found."

Luke 15:11-32

LAZARUS AND THE RICH MAN

There was a rich man who dressed in purple and fine linen clothes,
A beggar, Lazarus lay at his gates, among the dogs that licked his sores;
Then as time passed, Lazarus and the rich man died
Both men went to different places to reside;
Lazarus was carried to Abraham's bosom by angels, to rest and abode.

The rich man was buried, and in hell, opened up his eyes,
And saw far away, Abraham's bosom, with Lazarus inside;
He cried out: "Father Abraham have mercy on me," in his misery and shame
And asked to send Lazarus, to cool his tongue, from the agonizing flame;
Abraham said, there is no passage, for between them, a great fixed gulf divides.

Then he asked Him to send Lazarus to his five brothers, so they may repent,
And to testify to them, for fear they also will come into this place of torment;
They would listen, if Lazarus come to them from the dead, and appear
Abraham said, Moses and the prophets came, and they did not hear;
Neither will they be persuaded, if one who rose from the dead was sent.

Luke 16:19-31

81

Doris J. McMillan

ZACCHEUS

Zaccheus was a short man who stood low,
He lived in a town named Jericho;
Climbed a sycamore tree one day
To see Jesus passing that way;
But Jesus called for him to come down below.

Zaccheus came down out of the tree and rejoiced,
When Jesus selected his house to abide, as his choice;
That day upon his house came salvation
And he became a son of Abraham's nation;
Because the Son of Man had come to save a world lost.

Luke 19:1-10

FIRST MIRACLE OF JESUS

There was a marriage in Cana of Galilee, one of the best,
Jesus, his mother and the disciples were invited as quests;
When they wanted more wine, the mother of Jesus said, the wine has run out
Jesus said, "What have I to do with thee, my hour has not yet come about;"
Then his mother said to the servants, whatever he tells you, do as he requests.

There set two stone waterpots containing two to three-fourths of water apiece,
Which were used in the tradition of purifying the Jews, the highest to the least;
Jesus told them to fill the vessels to the brim
And when the water reached the top of the rim;
He commanded them to carry the wine to the govenor of the feast.

When the govenor tasted the wine that was transformed,
Your good wine was saved until now, to the bridegroom he informed;
They usually bring out the good wine first
And when men become drunk, they serve the worse;
The water made to wine was the beginning of miracles Jesus performed.

John 2:1-11

Doris J. McMillan .

NICODEMUS

Nicodemus, a Pharisee met with Jesus one night,
As a ruler of the Jews, he wanted to set the record right;
Rabbi, we know you are a teacher sent from God, he inquired
Because no man can do what you do, unless God desire;
Then Jesus began to teach him spiritual rebirth and insight.

A man must be born again to see the kingdom of God, Nicodemus was told,
Nicodemus asked, how can a man re-enter into his mother's womb, when he is
old?
Jesus said: "Except a man be born of the water and of the Spirit,
"He cannot enter into the kingdom of God," on his own merit;
Then Jesus' message on God's love for the world unfolded.

God loved the world so much; He gave His only Son,
On Whom the sins of the world were placed upon;
So those that believe on Him will not perish
But shall have an everlasting life to cherish;
For He was not sent to condemn them, but to save everyone.

John 3:1-17

THE SAMARITAN WOMAN

Jesus met a Samaritan woman in the middle of the day at Jacob's well,
She had come to draw water, not prepared for the story He had to tell;
Jesus said to her: "Give me to drink."
The woman did not know what to think;
For the Jews avoided the Samaritans, and the place where they dwelled.

Jesus said, If you knew the gift of God, and who you are speaking to,
And had asked him, he would have given living water to you;
The woman said to Jesus, "Sir thou hast nothing to draw with, and the well is deep"
Where is your living water? Are you greater than our father, Jacob that sleeps;
Who gave us this well, from which he, his children and cattle drank, and likewise we do?"

Jesus began to tell her of two types of waters, and said whosoever,
Drink of this well water will thirst, but the water that I give, will never;
Thirst or want for water again
There a well of water will be within;
Springing up into a life that will last forever and ever.

She asked for the living water, and truthfully answered Jesus, about her married life,
Jesus told her she had five husbands, and of the current one, she is not the wife;
When Jesus revealed Himself as the Messiah, she left her waterpot, and went her way
To tell the men in the city, to come see a man whom she had met that day;
That told her everything she had done, and asked, "Is not this the Christ?"

John 4:5-29

Doris J. McMillan

THE HELPLESS MAN

A certain man was sick for thirty-eight years,
Lay waiting to be placed in a pool, after an angel appeared;
Jesus saw him lying there, and stopped for a talk
He said: "Rise, take up thy bed and walk;"
Immediately the man arose, took his bed and walked without fear.

John 5:1-5

JESUS FEEDS FIVE THOUSAND

A great many people followed Jesus on his retreat,
Jesus asked his disciples about buying bread for them to eat;
Andrew saw a boy with two fishes, and five barley loaves of bread
Jesus took it, gave thanks, and five thousand men were fed;
Miraculously, they all were filled, with plenty left over of bread and meat.

John 6:1-13

Doris J. McMillan

LAZARUS RAISED FROM THE DEAD

A man named Lazarus became sick one day,
His sisters, Mary and Martha sent for Jesus right away;
Upon hearing the news he said: "This sickness is not for him to die
But that the Son of God might be glorified;
Stayed two more days, and preferred to delay.

When Mary saw Jesus, she fell at his feet and cried,
"Lord if you had been here, my brother would not have died;"
When Jesus saw her weeping, He wept, and His spirit groaned
"Look how He loved Lazarus," the others moaned;
Then they led his to the tomb of his graveside.

Jesus, along with Martha and others, went to Lazarus' grave,
Where a stone covered the entrance to the cave;
Jesus ordered them to take the stone away
Then spoke in a loud voice, and Lazarus, who had been dead four days;
Came out of the tomb in his graveclothes, on the command Jesus gave.

John 11:1-6, 32-44

BELIEVE IN THE LORD JESUS CHRIST

Jesus told his disciples not to trouble their hearts with despair,
If they believe in God, believe in Him, and made them aware;
That in His Father's house are many mansions
His words are the truth; they need no sanctions;
And a place for them He will go, and prepare.

Jesus said: "Believe on me and the works that I do,
So that you will be able to do the same thing too;
And anything you ask in my name, will be done
That the Father may be glorified in the Son;
Then a Comforter with the Spirit of Truth, I will send unto you."

John 14:1-3, 12-17

Doris J. McMillan

THE ANNOINMENT OF JESUS

Mary took a pound of expensive spikenard ointment,
Applied it to Jesus' feet, then wiped them with her hair in anointment;
"Why was not this given to the poor?" Judas asked in a sarcastic tone
Jesus said, "the poor will be with you always, leave her alone;"
For Mary had done this for His burial, and day of atonement.

John 12:1-8

THE CRUCIFIXION OF JESUS

Jesus came with a mission to fulfill,
To save the world from sin and to do his Father's will;
After enduring desertion, betrayal and denial
And false accusations at a degrading trial;
Completed the ultimate task at Calvary's hill.

Two thieves were crucified that day with Christ,
One questioned his authority, the other sought eternal life;
He said, "Lord when you come into your kingdom, remember me"
Jesus said, 'verily I say unto thee;
Today you shall be with me in paradise."

Joseph of Arimathaea went to Pilate to claim,
The body of Jesus, and placed it in a tomb where no one else had lain;
Pilate ordered the tomb sealed with a large stone and watched by guards
To secure and to keep Jesus' body inside;
But all of his orders were carried out in vain.

No longer was the world condemned and lost;
Because Jesus died upon Calvary's cross;
For the wickedness of man's behavior
Jesus Christ, our Lord and Savior;
Defeated Satan and showed him who's boss.

Mark 14, 15
Matthew 27:57-66

Doris J. McMillan

THE RESURRECTION OF JESUS

On the first day of the week, came three women who planned to care,
For Jesus' body, by anointing it with sweet spices, they had prepared;
Along the way they began to ask and say
"Who will roll the stone away?"
But on arrival, they found the tomb empty and bare.

A young man in a long white shining garment said, "Do not be afraid,
You seek Jesus, He is risen, look where He laid;
He has gone to Galilee
There He will be for you to see;
Go tell his disciples, he is risen from the dead."

Jesus Christ conquered death with his resurrection,
Believe on him and be saved, not face rejection;
But live and never die
And forever with Him reside;
In peace and everlasting perfection.

Mark 16

ASCENSION OF JESUS

The disciples asked Jesus, when will he again give Israel a kingdom and rebirth?
They were told only the Father knows the time, which is in His power of worth;
But they shall receive power after the Holy Ghost come
And shall go into Jerusalem, Judea, and Samaria and become;
Witnesses of him there, and into the uttermost parts of the earth.

After Jesus spoke those words, he was taken up in a cloud, out of their sight,
While the disciples looked up into the sky, two men stood by in clothing of white;
Asked, why are you gazing into heaven? This same Jesus you see ascending
Shall return unto you in like manner, descending;
As you see him now go up on his heavenly flight.

Acts 1:6-11

Doris J. McMillan

DESCENT OF THE HOLY SPIRIT

On the day of Pentecost, when they were all together in one place,
Suddenly, a sound came from heaven, a mighty rushing wind that raced;
Through the house, there sat upon them cloven tongues of fire
And they were filled with the Holy Ghost, as the Spirit gave desire;
For men of every nation to hear each other speak in his own language, face-to-face.

The Galileaens heard these men speak of God's wonderful works, and were amazed,
While others, confused by what they heard, had their minds in a cloudy haze;
Then astonishment and curiosity came into play
Causing some to doubt, and mockingly say;
These men are full of new wine and in a daze.

Peter stood up and let them know; these men do not speak in a drunken rave,
This was spoken of things to come in the last days, which the prophet Joel gave;
God's Spirit will be poured out upon all flesh; men and women will prophesy
Wonders and signs shall be shown in the heaven, earth, and the sky;
And those that call upon the Lord before His Great Day, shall be saved.

Acts 2:1-21

PETER HEALS A LAME MAN

A crippled man was carried daily to Beautiful Temple's gate,
And laid there in his weakened and disabled state;
He begged those entering into the temple for a donation
This was his way of earning a living, and making invocation;
Because from the time of his birth, his condition was innate.

When the man saw Peter and John about to go in, he made a request,
For gifts from them, to the betterment of his interest;
Both Peter and John with their eyes upon the man said, "Look on us"
The man paid attention to their words, and with trust;
Expected to receive something special, their very best.

Peter said, "Silver and gold have I none," What he had to give was not for fame,
"But such as I have, give I to thee, rise and walk in Jesus Christ of Nazareth's name;"
As he lifted the man up by the hand, his feet and ankles received strength
The man walked into the temple, praising God and leaping to great lengths;
And all who saw him, knew it was he, who once lay at the temple lame.

Acts 3:2-10

Doris J. McMillan

ANANIAS AND SAPPHIRA

Ananias and his wife, Sapphira sold their property of land,
Together, they devised a private cheating plan;
Ananias came to Peter, and without any discreet
Brought part of the money, and laid it at the apostle's feet;
Peter asked, "why has Satan filled your heart to keep the money beforehand?"

Peter asked, "while you had your property, was it not your own possession?
After it was sold, was not in your own power to act with repression?
Not only have you done this unto men, but unto God you have lied"
Then upon hearing these words, Ananias felled down and died;
And was carried out and buried by young men, who they heard the confession.

Later, Sapphira who was unaware of what had taken place, came inside,
Peter asked her, had she sold the land for a price? "Yes," she confided;
When he asked, had they both agreed together to hold in contempt
To show disobedience for the Spirit of the Lord, and to tempt?
She felled dead, and was carried out and buried by her husband's side.

Acts 5:1-10

96

PETER'S MIRACLE IN JOPPA

A certain disciple named Tabitha, which was called Dorcas by interpretation,
Lived in Joppa and did good works towards others, with consideration;
As it came to pass in those days, she became sick, and died
Her body was washed, and placed in an upper chamber; there it lied;
To wait for Peter, whom they had summoned hastily in desperation.

When Peter arrived, all the widows stood beside him and cried,
Brought and showed him coats Dorcas had made, before she died;
Peter kneeled and prayed, turned to the body and said, Tabitha arise
She opened her eyes; saw Peter, and sat up from her demise;
Then Peter took her by the hand, and presented her to the saints, "alive."

Acts 9:36-41

Doris J. McMillan

PAUL'S CONVERSION

On the way to Damascus, rode a man named Saul,
To persecute Christians with great gall;
But when Christ changed his ways
He preached the gospel all his days;
With a new name, not Saul, but Paul.

Acts 9

PAUL AND SILAS

Paul and Silas, two Christian men of long ago,
Spreaded the gospel as they traveled high and low;
With missionary work as their quest,
Healed the sick and the demon possessed;
When they spoke, evil spirits had to go.

Acts 16

Doris J. McMillan

PAUL AT MARS HILL

Paul stood on Mars Hill among men whose hearts were filled with superstition,
He saw written on the alter, "TO THE UNKNOWN GOD," this inscription;
Paul declared, the Lord of heaven does not live in temples made by hand
God made the world, all that is in heaven, in earth and upon the land;
Gave life and breath to all things, not to be ignorantly worshipped by a superscription.

Those who seek the Lord can feel and find Hm, He is not a thing,
For we live and move in Him, and are also His offspring;
Do not think of the Godhead as that of gold, silver, or stone chiseled by a device
Even in this ignorance, God commanded all men to repent, and He gave this advice;
On an appointed day, the world will be judged in righteousness, by Christ, Lord and King.

Acts 17:22-30

ARMOR OF GOD

Put on the whole armor of God, so you may be able to stand,
Against the tricks of the devil, and his demonic, army band;
We do not wrestle against flesh and blood
But against powerful rulers of darkness and its evil flood;
Of spiritual wickedness in high places at every hand.

Take with you the whole armor of God, to withstand in the evil day,
Stand with your loins fastened with truth, so you will not swag or sway;
Have on the breastplate of righteousness, feet with shoes prepared for peace
Above all, take the shield of faith, to have the fiery darts of the wicked cease;
With the helmet of salvation, the sword of the Spirit, and God's word; watch and
pray.

Ephesians 6:11-18

Doris J. McMillan

OUR HIGH PRIEST

Jesus Christ is our High Priest,
He loves all, the greatest to the least;
If we come to Him with confessions
Of our sins and transgressions;
He atones them and gives them peace.

Our High Priest after the order of Melchisedec,
Was Jesus Christ, let us not forget;
Who offered prayer and supplications
Obedience to God without hesitation;
Gave His life, for man's life was a wreck.

Hebrews 4:14-16, 5:5-10

JESUS, THE SACRIFICE

Jesus offered himself as sacrifice,
For sins of the whole world, not a slice;
When man could not be saved
By burnt offerings, or blood of animals so He gaved;
His life, the ultimate price.

Hebrews 10:1-14

Doris J. McMillan

FAITH

Faith is not made of things we see and hear,
But by the word of God, and not by the way things appear;
If we hope, obey, and believe
We will please Him, and receive;
A reward for our faith to seek Him without fear.

Hebrews 11:1-6

THE NEW JERUSALEM

In a vision, John saw a new heaven and earth, and there was no more sea,
The holy city new Jerusalem, descending from God, adorned as a bride to be;
Then a great voice from heaven said: "Look the tabernacle of God is with men."
They shall be His people, and He will dwell in them;
For God Himself will be in their midst, and they will forever be free.

Then God shall wipe away from their eyes, all tears,
And there shall be no more reason for sadness or fear;
No death, sorrow, crying, or pain
The former things will no longer remain;
And God upon the throne will make all things new and clear.

Then the voice said unto John, "It is done,
I am Alpha and Omega, the beginning and the end," the One;
Who will provide for those who are thirsty, and will freely give
A fountain of water from which to drink, and forever live;
And I will be his God, and he shall be my son.

Revelations 21:1-7

ABOUT THE AUTHOR

Doris Jean Davis McMillan was born in Wilmington, North Carolina. She is a former member of Shiloh Missionary Baptist Church in Wilmington, NC, and a current member of Antioch Missionary Baptist Church in Goldsboro, North Carolina. Her interest in poetry writing began in Antioch's Vacation Bible School in 1997. Since then, she has written poems about Sunday school lessons, members and their accomplishments, church organizations, and programs. Several poems about church events and members have been published in Antioch's newsletter, *The Benediction*.

McMillan is a high school graduate of Williston Industrial High School in Wilmington, North Carolina. She holds a Bachelor of Science Degree in Nursing, Norfolk State University, Norfolk, Virginia, and a North Carolina teaching license in Health Occupations.

She believes in the healing power of Jesus Christ, and has experienced His healing power in her life.

Printed in the United States
966400005B

9 780759 679436